POST-MORTEM OF THE EVENT

POST-MORTEM OF THE EVENT

KLARA DU PLESSIS

Copyright © Klara du Plessis, 2024
All rights reserved

Palimpsest Press
1171 Eastlawn Ave.
Windsor, Ontario. N8S 3J1
www.palimpsestpress.ca

Printed and bound in Canada
Cover layout and typography by Ellie Hastings
Edited by Jim Johnstone
Cover Artwork: Adam Basanta. *Split*. 2017. Mixed media.
Photo: Guy L'Heureux

Palimpsest Press would like to thank the Canada Council for the Arts and the Ontario Arts Council for their support of our publishing program. We also acknowledge the assistance of the Government of Ontario through the Ontario Book Publishing Tax Credit.

LIBRARY AND ARCHIVES CANADA CATALOGUING IN PUBLICATION

TITLE: Post-mortem of the event / Klara du Plessis.
NAMES: Du Plessis, Klara, 1988- author
IDENTIFIERS: Canadiana (print) 20240424476
             Canadiana (ebook) 20240424484

ISBN 9781990293771 (SOFTCOVER)
ISBN 9781990293788 (EPUB)
SUBJECTS: LCGFT: Poetry.
CLASSIFICATION: LCC PS8607.U17 P67 2024 | DDC C811/.6—DC23

CONTENTS

LIVE STREAM
    Dead air / 11
    .WAV / 27
    Sonnet overlay transcribed by https://otter.ai / 44
    The reading is a moment of hope— / 45
    Eros. Erratum / 52
    Uncompressed lyrical I / 53
    Gerund grid / 58
    Fonds / 64
    Of the giant trees, only the serpent remains / 66
    Breathe in scholarship / 71
    Ode of cracks / 81

THE EVENT
    Openwork / 85

POST-MORTEM OF THE EVENT
    Post-mortem of the event / 105

Notes / 113
Acknowledgements / 115
About the author / 117

To SpokenWeb

LIVE STREAM

Dead air

The linger poetics of the event is this:
(How long does it take to quell the spirit
if it isn't a question but a quest?)
The entire book is a rider
post-horseback, caught in the instant
it's flung into air with misspoken limbs.
In digital time, the posthumous speaker
spreads themself so thin, they're a specter
leaking diminuendo into the citation
of iambs. A tiny technology of sounding
out and the distance between each poem
is the revolutionary stasis of its pose.

Recording the event say, I am the event,
every line mics before and after the sonnet.

Every line mics before and after the sonnet.
Micro-sonic resonance of poetry.
Book history as scores, settled,
then resurrected as ongoing notation.
What has been written in the past exists
in the archive as a sequence of the present
and then as a prayer. Faint deity feints
in the metrical deception of temporality.
The vibratory track is always on. Click.
Sometimes the event can follow its footpath.
Afterlife *HLF*. It can reflect and refract.
But sometimes silence is its own searing static.

Verbal resolution of sounds, mouths,
open and amplified as words touching nouns.

Open and amplified as words touching nouns,
this is the event. Reclining anatomy, none
other than skin forward, stripped to the organ.
Nudity comes with the vibration of disrobing,
empty thrill of tactility, disclosing round
portals, no features, moon object of emotion.
First reader, like a fist of violin, says
she drowns in delight. Last reviewer suggests
Light, not the kind that spots an arena of activity,
but light that bursts in verbs of blind fury.
This sequence, this sequel, laser naked,
scaffolded in beams to make and remake.

No one clears the outcome, not even the event.
Throats as silk. Potential lauds out loud.

Throats as silk. Potential lauds out loud.
The internet, such a confident container
for monologues overlaid as polyvocal din.
Noise pollination meets heads that get work done.
Yes, this book will become other, will adapt.
Yes, transformation will be sound, meaning fit.
Yes, sound will lead to words, to text
so that process flourishes. Unwrite this book
in fluorescent flashing eye light.
A History of Light in full body glitter, glamour
synonymous with affirmation, confirmation
bias of absolute success and succession.

No professional receptacle beheads itself in scarves,
in verse cravats. Necks are the inverse of selves.

In verse cravats, inversions of self
are draped halfway between lungs and brow.
Inveigled in lauds loosened along the throat,
flattery of anatomy, from text to bowels.
In veil of silk, worms weave what used to be
skin and their doing, an undoing, an
invention of decomposition. Each larva
learns its own method of eating clean.
Inveigh the great death, rail against the break,
breath entering the body not through respiratory
tract, but through the vast ventilation of corpse.
Vainly, binding the poem in adoration.

I don't want to look like a bow, the event replies,
rhyme sutured to the front of every line.

Rhyme sutured to the front of every line
as symbolic reversal, no, as ′ ˘ ′ ˘ ′ ˘ ′ ˘
Teaching meter should be easy, trochees,
see. Here is the verse. Here is its beat.
Everything done by the event is patterned
in structure and yet. Repetition
of misrecognition of stressed, unstressed,
stressed leading to such tightness, frustration,
explosion, and all these little parts, shards,
significant others, tiptoed together, ripped
and rippling in untethered, unaccented ambition.
′ ˘ ′ ˘ ′ ′ ˘ A career move towards

beauty is such a heavy breath filigree river
pants off nudity free-for-all porno pure rigour.

Pants off nudity free-for-all porno pure rigour
this is all art the fear of producing nothing
of not being not being relevant enough
in the moment of seeing it could be rubbish
but roped in it is backside in white briefs dancing
why would this work be too sexual if woman
why is this suddenly about Plato's cave
with light and electronic music and play
how is it possible that writing pants off
earlier this morning the event knew to see
this video work knew it would be muscular lunar
incredible darkness in which eyes surge.

The ancient lady double crutches also looks
smiles hooked between us in recognition.

Smiles hooked between us in recognition
simile for the skin of small, sagging
breasts as they separate from chest to ball sacks,
no dicks. The difference between lie and lay
is doing and doing to. And the gay man
internal turned on by a straightness so vast.
This crown has been completely derailed.
Braid of father, son, and trial, final line and first,
a triptych surveillance, eyes hitched
to corners like baby heads emergent from thighs.
When permitted to sit, to watch, to glow, slowing
down the whole descent as surface, as slant dermis.

Art is a depth axis of skin or an archaic form
of being. The event not as hereditary hero.

The event not as hereditary hero,
but infant, swaddled in difference between
HLF, Light, and *A History of Light,*
between reception and receptacle, now and noun,
absorption and limit. At an event, the event
invokes Q&A so the author demands intro.
We've met many times. I am the event.
Instead the event defers. Lack leaks
down the immaculate poet. Time passes, the event
still thinks about this, disguising, not barking.
And then there's the mentor who creates
conditions to bring out the worst in the event,

adorned in hostility. No one hands out or permits.
Desire cites the courage to collapse the summit.

Desire cites the courage to collapse the summit.
Presence comes first into handwriting,
then into face, commitment to inhabiting
body. To inherit event and then submit
ƙpoq pronounced epoch into lingering.
Slow ease of almost moving. Negligee verse
stews in own filth, sweat, and gesture. No one
needs to be so sophisticated, they're unkind.
Bliss defecation, disentangling script in fragile
miracle of a molting spider's sustainability
limbs. The event's hands exist in reminiscence,
misspelling air as vast becoming. Credit

the crown as peak. From loss to life,
tempo hangs in limbo resilience close but not at

the edge. Tempo hangs in limbo resilience,
lances time in spikes, wrist resists wrists
chopping air in regular fast beat disco | | |
Can air glyph enough to erode the lyrical,
to object event into rhythm? *A History
of Light* is l|||ght drawn out as perpendicular
futurity. This is unwritten, unperformed.
The question without mark. The cursor
without blink | | | still, wraparound
series, sequel, sequence billows and then
intimates defeat after the nth fight, after
I becomes duration. Sky buckles

so curvature and connection slot metal
skeleton into slow horizontal   –·

Skeleton is slow horizonal   –·   –· · ···
skid chassis loses grip of ideas when that idea
(singular) is doubling down rather than giving in.
Now giving is a kindness to ease, to interiority.
HLF's obsession with hell as light,
and skin as sound blasting from within:
page, screen, laptop draft, reality. Loosening
to site-specific self-excavation, a dig
so deep it relayers, leaves one round womb
to dot the skyline underground.
i is the event's unknown and -i is ellipsis
to plural, suffice it to say, a suffix.

 . . . .:::::::::::⋮⋮⋮⋮⋮⋮⋮⋮ Stillness semblance inertia
if life after death means repetition.

If life after death means repetition
of redness, the event suspects cartilage
nesting in its afterlife. Ossification leafage.
What's visible is mobility, quickening
of beaks. Slender leakage from anatomy
to grey drainage of tight, triangular bird lips
dipped in plumage. Speak from the chest
no song but the clearest meaning, a message cast,
a whole parliament of sonnets: twist
the couplet's doubling act, reflect on infinity
full tilt, notate the sepia gaps, gaping, escaping
the bleeding heart flora of the everything life.

High-coloured, flushed hereafter, humiliation
death, oh darling, darling discography, dear air.

Dear air,
this monologue is a microphone,
XLR cables coiling down, performance
of breath. Weft of strophes undone.
Poetry weeps beyond each deceased line
break. Enjambment claustrophobia.
So the event rehearses the event and in
that knowledge of redoubled effort, invokes
oxygen so the tongue's sunset
aspirates into void rigid lungs,
instils ambition in the muscle of rhyme.
Final exhalation ex nihilo. Lectern demise

displaces lecture hall for editing, aerating,
open mouth murmur, murder of dead air.

The linger poetics of the event is this:
every line mics before and after the sonnet,
open and amplified as words touching nouns.
Throats as silk. Potential lauds out loud.
In verse cravats, necks are the inverse of selves,
rhyme sutured to the front of every line.
Pants off nudity free-for-all porno pure rigour
smiles hooked between us in recognition
of being. The event, not the hereditary hero,
desires, cites the courage to collapse the summit.
Tempo hangs in limbo resilience close but not at
the edge. Skeleton is slow horizonal   –.
if life after death means repetition.

Oh darling, darling discography, dear air,
open mouth murmur, murder of dead air.

The linger poetics of the event is this:

open mouth murmur, murder of dead air.

.WAV

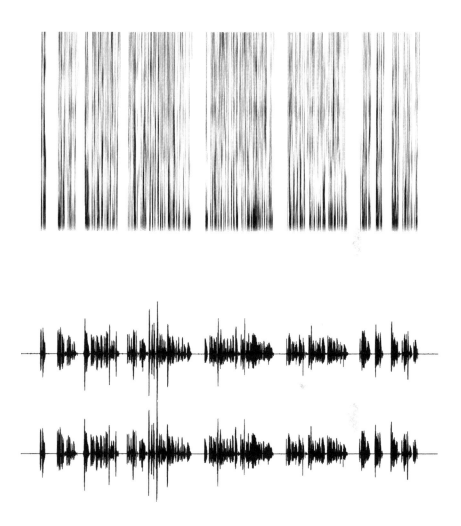

Sonnet Annotation 1: Sound wave form

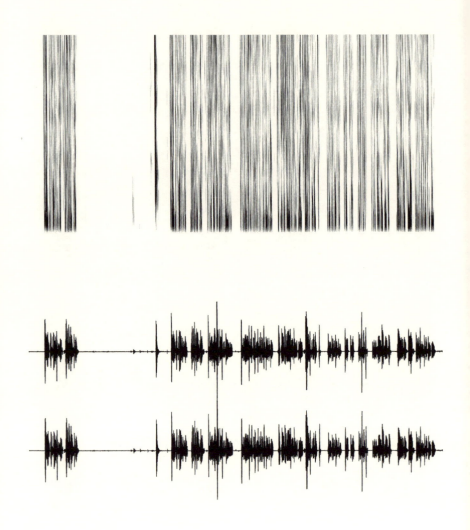

Sonnet Annotation 2: A small sound

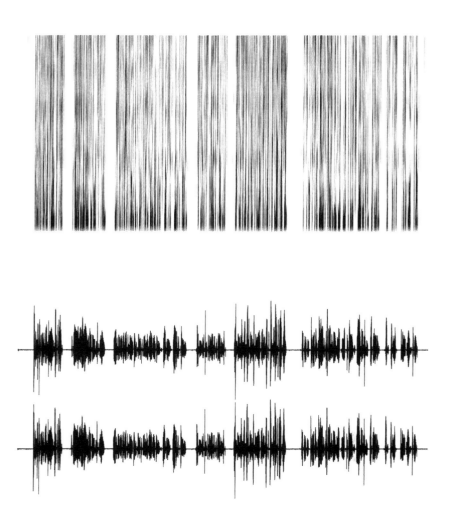

Sonnet Annotation 3: Pun on spectral spectrogram

Sonnet Annotation 4: Uncompressed lyrical I

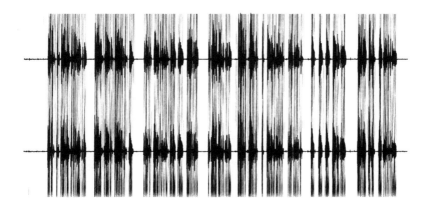

Sonnet Annotation 5: Signal to noise topos

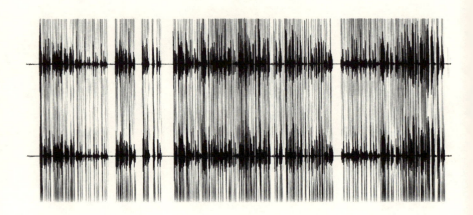

Sonnet Annotation 6: Poetic zipline, wave topography

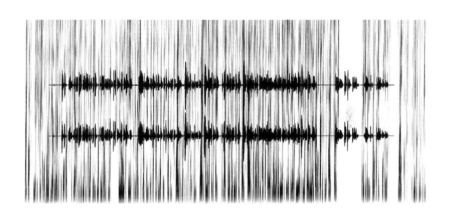

Sonnet Annotation 7: The rise, parallel sound wave barcode

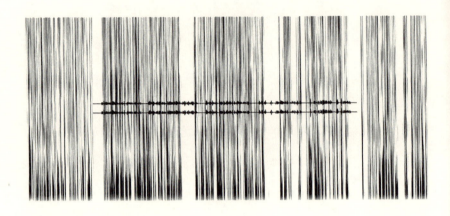

Sonnet Annotation 8: Contracted barcode, water weave, event

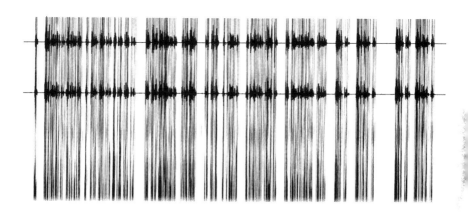

Sonnet Annotation 9: Lowtide

Sonnet Annotation 10: Mobility, hips forward

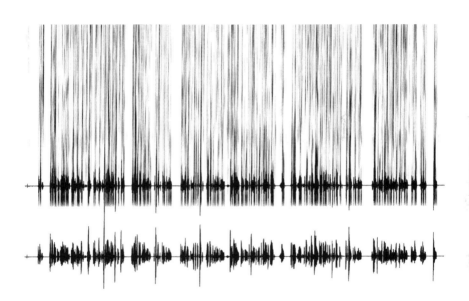

Sonnet Annotation 11: Hightide

Sonnet Annotation 12: Froth

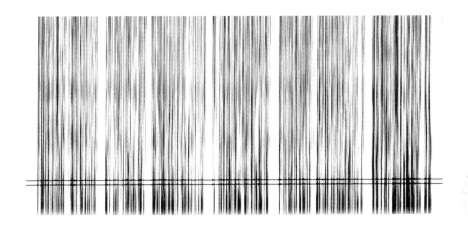

Sonnet Annotation 13: Oceanic fray

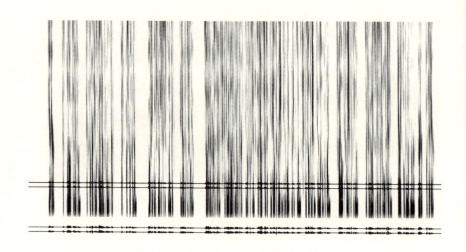

Sonnet Annotation 14: Line in the sand

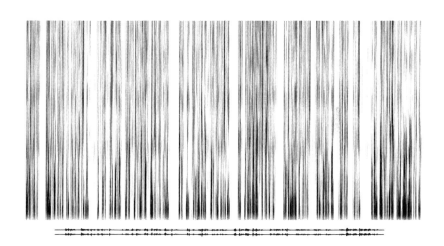

Sonnet Annotation 15.1: Tiny ripple.WAV

Sonnet Annotation 15.2: Waves.WAV

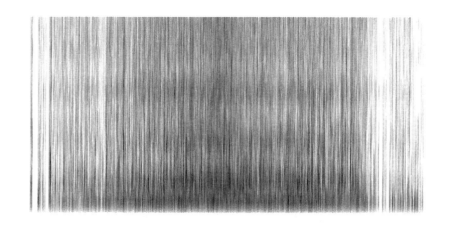

Sonnet Overlay: Gale force

Sonnet overlay transcribed by https://otter.ai

00:00:02   Dead air. The linger poetics of the event is this line. Die. Take off. Boiling isn't a question, but micro-sonic. Town, post-horseback, caught in the other universe. Internet of cells in relation to trust.

00:00:33   Every year.

00:00:45   Why? About

00:00:57   to find

00:01:13   out. Ready,

00:01:37   horizontal desire. If life after death, stillness. If life, darling as fuck.

Darling discography, dear air, open mouth murmur, murder of dead air.

The reading is a moment of hope—

Death dons a family meeting,

confinement of life

in reverse,

version

cataplectic.

Every skulking member sucked back into the womb,

where the worm is the tomb.

Read last rites.

Stravinsky

of energy

sharp

nervous

bursts

beckon to a frantic, unfinished, panic-stricken clasp

at life-before-death.

Role of this get-together

is the funereal,

the fun in the unreal.

There is so much sadness in each unit of humanity, un- becomes it

as in, sadness becomes humanity

or sadness suits mortality.

Morality is not the terrain of the hereafter.

Orality tantrum

greases the pan before public decease.

One body is teeth and one body is bitten.

This is the model of error

or

the o of apostrophe,

the straw seen from above

in the instant before squeezing between. Dental

inhalation,

airborne agenda

in elegy.

Horizontal holy ghost beast march

overpowers cruising for crusades.

Even democracy parades across the globe as if

on demand.

Secular religion, still religion.

Humanitarian, still humanity.

Return mankind to the animal table vibe.

Books on top.

Books inside.

Ass open like a paperback.

The closest approximation to book is boo.

Scary,

all this galloping to the races of a good life.

When loved ones pass

and all that's left is beauty,

complexity eclipsed by lipping sonics

oblivion to obvious optics

sweat water to sweet water.

It sucks.

The uncontrollable grief of everything that was meant to be.

Death.

Hate.

Pig-eyed love.

Blood on the amour abattoir.

Diminuendo of ego.

War.

Illness.

Defeat.

The indecipherable fight. Infidelity

as the dopamine of disappointment.

Nuclear is both single family

and figuration of hitting the roof big time.

Edit this satire to satyr.

That guy has a tail and ears. It's normal to have ears.

That guy has horns. Isn't it normal to be born?

Bomb

the bad boy genre.

Just once walk into the room with anger.

The event has a strong center.

Camo fermata.

Camel ⌒ ⌒ insert.

Chameleon spells breasts with inverted nipples.

Listen.

This is a poetry reading.

Everyone dying

can live safely in the metaphor of their hope

in the hop-hoop-hoopla-hula hoop

knowledge

that the screen's shot through with ammo

that the live stream is always off by a fraction of time,

that the war ended later in Africa,

enough to warp any illusion of intimacy, of immediacy,

of saying *is* without *to be*.

Tubular volume gauge

of this sound editing software

pumps

decibels in the lowest-fi animation of desire.

Flicker of energy in oblong proportions,

pink annexation

lands decay

on rocks

on planets

orbits plumping with want.

Sound waveform of this poem

spikes in

militaristic precision

medicinal optimism.

The animal roar

raw war

careering forward

into battle

into playback

garlanded present

fluorescent flowers

soldiers in laurels

soldered with rose hips

Eros. Erratum

Think back less
than a hundred years when humanity loved progress.

Imagine the solace of feeling right.
Now crawl

Uncompressed lyrical I

The event's become so accustomed to not belonging

that the event's forgotten how to belong.

belonging

belong'ing

belon'nging

belongi'ng

belongi'nging

belongi'm

belongi've

belongi'd

belongit's

belongin't

Can I just say—this is the event on the line—Inglish—
-i'nglish—less used suffix that means to belong.

-ing

i'ng

I'ng

I ing

Iing

-Ing

One belonging.
Two belongings.

What is the difference between I
and —

Gerund grid

The line and the angle are at odds.

Angular dimensions, holding.
Angular structures, including.
Angular embraces, space.

To be inside the right angle is to reside outside.
Perhaps.
Everything is a matter of perspective, and that perspective is not an experience of unit and measurement.
Living breathing enjambment.

Place rectangular importance over the event.
Now it is a page.
A work.
A window. Unless it's a round window, an eyeing,
since to be round the window emulates the iris.
Seen in profile, the eye is
shaped like a drop, leaking a tear in side-eye.
The eye-shaped window looks at the event,
longs
for the sharp corners of a room,
purges its purpose with poets.

Stretch the canvas like a pose | like a posy
prostate
for the angled finger to scroll through joyously.

Soon the event pronounces its fame.
It alights,
light-footed and heady. It opens
its mouth for other poems to open theirs,
to open theirs,
so throat becomes a mouth
and stomach becomes a mouth
and intestinal gut health becomes a mouth.

The event wants a constant entering.
To enter and enter and enter
the performance
to activate, to cheer, to yes,
to find surface beneath surface, to find surface above surface
porous entering aerating
deepening
opening
slackened jaw for recitation.

The recreational poem recreates,
rehearses, recites.

Sight is wet because eyes do not dry. There is no sun
in a room called a hall, not a hallway traversing into further rooms,
but a hall, a compression
with doors always departing. If the doors are a perforation of the angular
why is the exit strategy always to exit?

Exist.

Now rectangular bed endowed with linen and down
comfort my yearning,
come forth into the morning
when everything releases against the boxy edges of day and night.
The three-dimensional rectangle imprints its frame, a faint outline
onto everything that curves or frays.
Still, the poetic line doesn't stray.
It tightens itself, salutes the sun,
opens its chest,
armed with weights,
weaponizing the expediency of strength.

Replicate space angled with time folded like a sieve.

Transparent rectangle of the medium
places itself over the event,
unseen.

Unseemly yet seamlessly
there. Present, impressing itself onto air.

Fray can be an unruly congregation.
Fray can be the unravelling of the stretch. Empty form still
hovers with the insinuation of its purpose
and the gerund grid
wings its own expanse

Fonds

Acclimatizing to bondage
this fonds
sails into language with mispronunciation and absence.
How to even say it—

Incremental information breaks down into sections and sub-
missive sections. Don't blame the messenger
winged sandals, Achilles heel and all. The archive
divides into files numbered Hermes, Hermes Trismegistus, and scarves.
Another composite of tradition and silk.
Boundaries tighten into ever smaller categories.
The restraints erupt maniacally, then the pink
partitions of pleasure, facets of the long fuck,
plucked from the partial anatomy of some god.
Mythology is the fundament of all risk,
fact
with its tendency towards the linear, practically invented kink.

Contrary to etymology, perversion
is really just the most direct obsession with a single unit,
or the obvious made nubile. Put
that in my file.

Languages jump into each other at the same rate
that one language colonizes every place,
thing, person, document, and I wish ellipses weren't dead to me.
Composed, soft repose,
verbose sentinels of knowledge. No. Messaging
shifts into sentiments of vibrancy,
but even when up close, the hyperlink, the searchability,
the activated process is a matter of language,
of redefining the body of work that lies quietly
hoping to be worshipped,
derived,
analyzed with cords,
in complete stasis

Of the giant trees, only the serpent remains

I stop
to think of the magnitude of the male body,
then the delicacy of buttons.
The precision of a button's edge, weighted and expanded
to parachute
to open its chest
beyond the slit of a garment.

Little packet of reserve buttons and yarns,
noting the item it belongs to. If one day it perforates.
Light pink and mother of pearl.
Variegated and mute.
I have never affixed these darlings to my clothes, needle
screaming through fabric and the faraway reaches of air.

Canopy of the sublime
inhale me,
cloth copy of expanding chest, an invocation
to soft, exquisite blasphemy.
Gentle molecule threaded through with hormonal thrust.
The thick morality of hetero days in which the maternal premise uncoils.

By chest is meant chest, breastplate,
the flat horizon of the geometric body, poles and lines.
When I say I would make a handsome man,
he suggests my shoulders are too small and I imagine saluting
the portrait of my body
in heroic pose
museum body for posterity
poster boy of voluminosity.

A collapse of men is a group formation
not intended as generalization but intended
as image.
Those paintings of inferno or purgatory or hell
or the world opening to swallow its sinners as they tumble red
head over heels down the aching hills of paradise.
Men, and women as men,
muscles, a cascade of romance
rippling but ripped in the imaginary downpour of immorality.

The lack of descriptor bothers me
and as usual the dictionary doesn't help.
It's not a collapse, not a caving in.
The mobility of pouring, but sharpened.
Pine for the fury of distortion.
Opine language with its inability to access omniscience.

O sublime twist of this poem,
forgive my adjacencies. Kneeling's not sufficiently prostrate
to beg the vocabulary of being.
I stretch out along the floor, arms aloft but horizontal,
legs long and pointed with muscles alert,
surfacing my back.

Optical invocation of the seen.
Regal adulation of the unknown.
It feels like I know
the heritage of kings and queens,
but really I'm stuck looking at the broken brocade of artworks
virtually presented
bewildered and in wonderment at lace.

I sublimate the idea of a wraparound gown
into an embrace, wrong,
into clips
locked in with a pop
this modern technology of regalia.

Hurtled through the still,
this moving image reminds me these bodies
warped in their own cavernous decline,
torn apart in cohesion,
merely emulate the folds
of some unnamed monarch's hoop
dress. Following the velvet's welcoming gesture
into ungrammatical stasis
the long recline
the drape
I flow

Breathe in scholarship

Docudrama of the folder, the file
cabinet, the archive
enlivened by the trickle of drawers sliding open with facts.
Then the drop, the letting go,
the ever-unspooling emotion rippling or ripping
information
with tension.

Facts as coagulated nervousness
preside in reason.

Anxiety
is an axis
where hands engage themselves—
ringing, yes, but wringing
out the policies of the head. Seep of thought.
Hands knot into catacomb.
That is one solution. Or
hands wind up the air like dolls touch-
ing the wide expanse of separation, or
the openness synonymous with connection.

Nothing, a moth grammatically remade as gerund,
fluttering with suffixes,
suffice it to say
nervousness is an emptiness splintering into ever littler
fragments of affect.

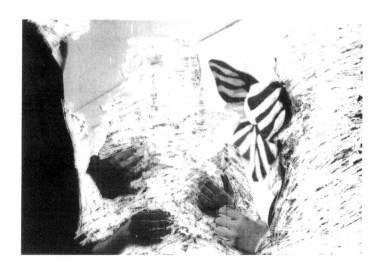

Document After the Fact 1

Hands bandage the air in self-inflicted microaggressions.
Microphones pad the selfsame air with phonemes.

Punctuate the self with hands
so that fact persists after the fact, a procession
racing over and erasing itself in the new fixity of telling the happening.

This is a document of affect. This is a document after the fact.
The document documents
the event, which is itself documents
document-
ing.

Craft of reconstructing
happening into what happened, with the pretension of activating.

The archive in its close proximity to exhibition,
deadhouse, or dormitory, hobbyist
of linearity—
the negativity of these lines misleading.

Files are for folding an endlessly long repertory—

Event links to document—links to archiving—links to
file—links to search criteria—links to reuse value—links to
download—links to print—links to poem, in time—

Document After the Fact 2

Working together splinters.
Writers on plinths
recline in upright postures or upside down fetuses,
feet structured in collaboration.

Duct taping persons into sculptures—
when to use people
when to use persons

Use can be the simple structure of a verb
or the complex structure of exploitation.
Used to can be the past
or habituated familiarity of repetition.
Use is but a suffix away from *us*, a deletion from *u*,
collaborative pronoun
you, reader,
and us,
attending,
attending to.

Shadow usurps.
Sharp flex.
The closed document, illegibly overcast,
covers shut like blackout curtains or weighted blankets,
the kind of auditorium darkness
that clasps the suspenseful inhale of velvet and dust.
Hyperventilating at home in bed as a kid, overstimulated by event,
seeing right through the blind out onto the street
which is nighttime at its most unknown.

Gown of sleep, perform me, uncouth and ungenerous as memory.

Document After the Fact 3

Us is a substitution away from *un-*
from one
unit.

Storage unit,
scourge of levity,
dominant in any power play.
The dark glamour of discovery distinguishes past tense
as tension rather than tensity.
Nervousness dissolves its plasticity,
a mold of the same and the same and the same.

Even in interpretation the equation of selfsame forgets the self.
The hole, whether a pore or the entire world, is for moving through

Ode of cracks

Origin is not the start.
Order disambiguates.
A sudden drop of petals wills the wilting bouquet to surface.
Take these cut flowers in their new role as bouquet,
flourishing backwards to the plant, shoot, root,
to the seed, earth, prominence in a previous arrangement.

The principle of provenance
relates to a preconceived rationale of traces.
The box of documents left in rubbish state stays
that way, is the order of things | fins | fabulous decay.
When the flowers drop is whatever,
but the trajectory from stem to table
of contents is preordained, a perfect, archival rationale.
Roots are nonsense, till they haunt for eternity.

Genesis always slips one step beyond its own definition
reimagining the provenance of poetry,
the randomness of style,
the ancestry of documents.
Speech act of the torso, settled in its plinth or vase
fainting forward to the floor | poem | immortal resting place of literature.

Roll up logic like a scroll, fount of pride and knowing, immolated and nil.
Compose an ode of cracks. Reel, reeling in the beginning of going

THE EVENT

Openwork

00:00:00	Thank you for being here.
	Thank you
	[…]
00:01:24	culture
	culture
	[…]
00:04:02	basically just saying
	I just want to say
	maybe one other thing
	[…]
00:06:02	that
	that's
	[…]
00:06:27	voice is adult
	voice adults
	[…]
00:07:18	now
	now
	now
	[…]

00:08:08   very
                  very
                  [...]

00:08:37   the dust will settle
                  the dust
                  the dust settling
                  [...]

00:11:06   stop there

00:00:00 The event, ~~a diversity of voices to hear from or dislike. However, it is marketing. The writing style which happened to be narrative is entered here to celebrate stories.~~

00:04:02 ~~I just want to say maybe one other thing. I wanted to stay very free. It has three sections. The middle section is about heart, identity, creativity. The first nuclear metal section, an intro. And then the two framing sections are fragmentary. Relationships~~ event. ~~The final or last section is emotion. First century punishment.~~

00:27:40 There's this great event. ~~Come the aggressors! It certainly was during women's stay at home. They manipulate power. Itself scary. The violence you could get held up in. You have to be ready for it, to get called up to fight, to survive. That's the language they use. So if that's the forehead, where does that get paid back? Just perpetuated.~~

00:33:07 ~~Despite the silence,~~ eventually.

01:15:58 ~~It gets a lot, yeah. I think there's something to be said for being so impersonal. Yeah,~~ it's not a reading event?

00:08:37	What to do with knowledge. To carry myself up through armfuls of velvet. Dust will settle so I'm jumping straight into the dust settling in the corners of the grid. Don't worry. No worries. That dust just never corners. Red waiting. My eyelash instantly itemizes my eyelash, my opinion, man. I believe in excuses, like death. Enter an eyelash parenthesis, raised metrically.
00:10:57	Uneven beauty.
00:11:06	Okay I'm going to stop there
00:11:23	because it is narrative and the first time that I've really been there. I realized at some point that I don't do character. I am a fiction writer and novelist. Am I not? The narrative too is very much based on interiority. So you get all of that landscape, all of those internal thoughts going on and images coming up. Part of the writing process was brilliant. I don't know how to write. I don't know how to make it happen. How do you get someone that's interesting? How do you get someone to see that everyone's muttering?
00:13:16	I don't know who spoke.

00:14:13	If this was set in a novel, I don't think there would be action, so let me live inside.
00:15:45	It's in the work. We find those who understand.
00:15:57	Find out what that looks like and what that feels like.
00:16:44	It was created, this particular scenario.

00:17:04   an erotica

00:17:19   or rotting

00:17:33   these eras

                 [these ears]

00:19:14	In this [that] entire book, I never talked about South Africa. I never mentioned it. I never stated in an entire book, the background.
00:20:15	You can always reflect that you're not neutral.
00:20:22	Right, right, there's the whole multiplicity of violence.
00:20:47	Violence is under the surface.
00:22:05	Voice is so much bigger.
00:26:55	I didn't know what to expect. I can see your voice and your voice is the violence.
00: 27:40	There's this great event. Come the aggressors! It certainly was during women's stay at home. They manipulate power. Itself scary. The violence you could get held up in. You have to be ready for it, to get called up to fight, to survive. That's the language they use. So if that's the forehead, where does it get paid back? Just perpetuated.

00:28:46   I've prepared a transcript to face in advance. It's more about art violence, like sagging into a squat. Lay down the law of use. There is a small group of pain. Find a fatality and make use of modulation. Sorry. Here. I keep wanting to make a cursory reading of this series. It's so hot, so hot. Artists are taking matters into your own hands. Open. The sounds and vibrations. Take a shot at the past. You have an identity adjuster between the arguments.

00:31:27   Graciously spy, in a manner planned, working your eyes. To see warm, ovulating irises grow into straight gardens. Enjoy life, elaborating everything. Seems to work.

00:32:10   I guess the question is, how the violence we're talking about branches into malaise in relation to unthinking violence.

00:32:38   Creation and interconnectivity.

00:33:07   Despite the silence.

00:33:07   Despite the silence—

00:34:21	I feel
00:34:23	tender because you're critically engaged.
00:35:07	I always think about these kind of comments. You know, a lot of artists are political, but then you look at the circumstances.
00:36:28	There's colour in that space. At first, there's every colour, there's the whole colour wheel, or the full use of colour, but then there's the use of colour to achieve effects of authority in that middle section.
00:42:41	I was creating a narrative.
00:42:47	It's overlaid with background
00:43:00	where people are sometimes allowing themselves to be seen. Sometimes naming things is doing the same, like not having it all be seen.
00:43:18	A name can be really loaded. It can be so loaded that it's painful. I got my own kids with a fucking nightmare. You have to name a total disaster. If you spend a lot of time with various storylines, or you spend a good chunk

	of time in movies, one of the first questions that you get is your family name. You have to have a sense of where we're at. So. Yeah. South Africa. Backgrounds. It's actually not even
00:44:49	this sort of violence.
00:52:49	Makes me wonder if we're getting to a place that is either cultural or character. They've gone through forms of violence or whatever. Look where that is, what their voice was. Saying that beauty can come with a wave, I actually find that violent. Yeah, because pretty is hard.
00:53:52	Saying that beauty can come with a wave, I actually find that violent. Yeah, because pretty is hard.
00:56:37	I went to South Africa and I started walking around the city a lot. Beautiful. Really lovely. Beautiful. Terrible things, but this beauty, so beautiful.
00:57:18	At various points, your work is beautiful. Sometimes beauty in its totality is like a blade of grass, playing breezy. We can find different ways not to be a bad person or word.

00:48:47   Me and, say, beauty. Branded nature. Somebody like green. You're right in this rotation. It's partly morale. Ugly, the smiling. This is physical. Stop me. Blah, blah, blah. I want to connect back to what you were talking about. This ontological question of making art, consent to its use by the artist. The segment we're talking about. Power and aging and symbology. Using these materials is about having a shared cultural meaning and that's about it. The code that's shared. Where does that overlap with appropriation? That which is very much an idea. The use of materials that are supposed to be from a shared cultural heritage, but then who shares in that? Who shares ritual? You're thinking about that in terms of Christian ideology. The family unit. The construction imposing itself in her area. There's so much overlap because it brings to mind the idea of degenerate art. Many have idolized the classical idea of beauty and put that on a pedestal, only for the beautiful surface to hide this terrible, terrible ugliness beneath it. So sometimes the aesthetic is just this video. Stasis. As a writer, somebody would tell you about beauty or soul or all these various things that you love to have in your work. I had to really think about why I was there and what it meant in my own work. I remember reading an interview with this artist and she said something along the lines of, well, people don't want you to have access or don't want you to write about beauty or think about beauty. It's pointless. It's not doing a service. It's the same reason why people you know may criticize and then take care of people. Your people. Very actively right about beauty as method. It's a thing to pay attention. Yes. Exactly. Exactly. Yeah. Yeah. Makes me wonder if we're getting to a place that is either cultural or character. They've gone through forms of violence or whatever. Look where that is, what their voice was. Saying that beauty can come with a wave, I actually find that violent. Yeah, because pretty is hard.

00:11:08 00:11:23 00:16:44 00:19:14 00:21:26 00:21:53
00:23:04 0023:22 00:24:44 00:25:27 00:26:14 00:27:40
00:28:46 00:35:07 00:35:53 00:36:51 00:39:07 00:39:53
00:40:16 00:42:41 00:43:21 00:46:31 00:56:22 00:56:37
00:57:18 00:58:19 00:59:38 01:02:30 01:06:28 01:10:28
01:12:29 01:14:57

    kind

    of

01:17:36   Lyrical,
                my poem.
                By poem.
                […]

01:18:10   Sorry.
                I'm sorry.
                […]

01:18:30   Friendly.
                You just look friendly.
                […]

01:18:33   I know.
                Often dogs identify me as a dog,
                a fellow dog,
                tall dog.

00:00:00   place
   –   place
01:18:33   palace
                 replace
                 places
                 places

00:00:00   o

00:00:00   o   o   o   o
                  o   o
                           o
                  o   o
                  o
                                        o
                        o   o   o
                        o   o   o

00:00:00   o   o

00:00:00
                        o
                  o
                  o   o
                  o
                  o   o   o o   o
                  o   o
                                  o   o
                        o   o o   o   o   o
                           o   o   O
                              o   o
                        oo   o   o
            o   o   o   o
            o
            o   o   o
                              o
                  o   o
                        o   o
                           o   o   oo   o   o

00:00:00   o   o   o
                o
         o   o   o   o   o

POST-MORTEM OF THE EVENT

Post-mortem of the event

The event lies on the table with its left hand and frontal
arm dissected.
Sinews and muscles and maybe one disposable bone
strumming, lines from a poem.
Pink inner exposé rationalizes the soul
from vessel to enlightenment, the latter so mystical
who knows how the verse becomes a multi-dimensional grid.

Logic of the luminous skin
of the other hand, intact, pale ram's brawn
of the Cartesian | Caucasian corpse

The event
opened, undocumented archive over the table,
displayed | splayed | played
anatomically laid out to rest | resist
Laboratory pages white as coats.

Only thing
is that the left hand is not the left,
but the right,
but not the right hand,
but a second right hand
multifarious body mirroring itself in hands.
In hand, rippling along its definitions of progress, usage, and control.
On the one hand and on the other hand as wingspan.
On the one hand and on the one hand, or
on the other hand and on the other hand.

The archive of hands fans out,
fingers replicating
selves.
Look. Really look
at this artwork so strange, armoured in mourning like the night.

Some look rationally, some at the event, some look nowhere in particular.
But here it's less about the gaze,
more about the circular pink cheeks clapped by hands
not applauding, but astounded.
Ashamed by the invasion.

The event notes
the method of laying a little cloth over the groin as if a collar.
Moratorium of
oral poem
not unspoken
but spoken with the outside of the mouth,
with the dexterity of bone.

The outside of the mouth is its own apparatus
including cheekbones, microphones, wires,
and speakers.
No one says a thing and yet is speaking,
hardwired to emit electricity as sound. Loudspeaker softened to speaker,
speaker guarding the event with salience | silence

The speaker continues to speak from outside the head
reverse engineering the outer brain of everything
towards the inner brain of everything
sonic trajectories,
arrows,
darts,
delicatessens,
treats rolling around the mouth.

The event sends a pic of a chocolate bar to a friend
and the friend sends the exact same pic back.
Got to go for a walk. Got to go for a run.

The event starts over, with emotion
searches:
the almond-shaped mass inside the head | hand
finds:
body background monochrome
searches:
grey matter
finds:
dark tissue of nerves
searches:
short branched extension
finds:
cells | self
searches:
synapse
finds:
junction
searches:
neural
finds:
cerebral.
The only reason for writing is pure ecstasy.

When upright, standing, air is the table the event lies back on.
When strobe lights fondle the crowd,
every figure is momentarily stuck in posture,
in the strangeness of anatomy
with eight men and an extra dead
struck still in time
in the instant
before darkness hits
before bodies speed up
moving
the event
rapid-fire, risqué
rinsing themselves in light
and a handshake with air

NOTES

1. "Dead air": A crown of sonnets conceptually based on the interconnection of *HLF* (or *Hell Light Flesh*, 2020), its adaptation as an opera-film called *Light* (Jimmie LeBlanc, Michael Hidetoshi Mori, 2023), and a still unwritten sequel projected as *A History of Light*.

   "I don't want to look like a bow" is a statement gleaned from a toddler. Thank you, Anaya Hussain.

   The seventh sonnet engages with Wolfgang Tillmans' 2015 single channel video work, *Instrument*.

2. ".WAV": A sequence of sound wave visualizations and spectrograms created using Praat. The visualizations are based on sound recordings of "Dead air." Thank you to SpokenWeb for the use of their recording studio at Concordia University.

3. "Fonds": In archival work, *fonds* is a grouping or folder of documents that share the same origin.

4. "Breathe in scholarship": I created the three images in 2013. The images are reworked photo-documentation from a chamber opera called *Photo Socrates*, performed at the Nikki Bogart Verein, in Vienna, Austria, on 26 October 2012. I wrote the libretto and Clio Montrey composed the musical score.

5. "Ode of cracks": In archival work, the *principle of provenance* implies that records of items must be created in the same order in which they were received.

6. "Openwork": A processual poem. In September 2020 during the COVID-19 pandemic, I launched *Hell Light Flesh* in Montreal's Parc Jarry, inviting three groups of five persons to discuss the book with me. Each meeting was based on reading the same extracts from *Hell Light Flesh,* started with the same introductory comments, and were directed by the same questions. "Openwork" functions as the three audio recordings of these discussions, overlaid on GarageBand and then transcribed using otter.ai. It is thus based on a nonsensical text that converges on axes of similar themes and keywords. With thanks to Oana Avasilichioaei, Ali Barillaro, Aaron Boothby, Alexei Perry Cox, Robin Durnford, Dean Garlick, Julia Konow, Jessi MacEachern, Rachel McCrum, Katherine McLeod, Erín Moure, James O'Callaghan, Matt Poole, and Emma Telaro for their participation.

7. "Post-mortem of the event": This poem engages with Rembrandt Harmenszoon van Rijn's 1632 painting *The Anatomy Lesson of Dr. Nicolaes Tulp.*

ACKNOWLEDGEMENTS

Thank you to the Canada Council for the Arts for their financial support of this book.

Four poems from "Dead air" were published as "Dead air: Four sonnets from a crown" in *The Stinging Fly*, Issue 49:2, Winter 2023-2024.

"Post-mortem of the event" was recorded and released as a lathe-cut vinyl record in a limited edition of 2 copies, produced by Angus Tarnawsky for SpokenWeb.

"Of the giant trees, only the serpent remains" was published as "Sublime curlicue" in *Oomph!: Contemporary Works (Vol. 3), A Multilingual Anthology*, 2022.

"Fonds" and "Ode of cracks" were published as "Fonds" and "Principle of provenance" in *The Stinging Fly*, Issue 46:2, Summer 2022.

"Fonds" was released as a limited edition broadside of 10 copies with Anstruther Press, 2021.

"Breathe in scholarship" was published with scholarly annotations as "Archiving anxiety" on the *Canadians Read* website, 2021. This publication formed part of a mentorship program with Gregory Betts, organized by Paul Barrett and Sarah Roger.

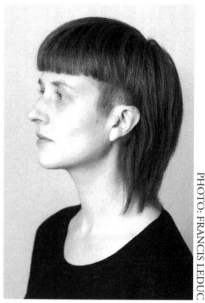

PHOTO: FRANCIS LEDUC

Klara du Plessis is a poet, artist-scholar, and literary curator. Her debut poetry collection, *Ekke,* won the 2019 Pat Lowther Memorial Award and her critical writing received *Arc Poetry Magazine*'s 2022 Critic's Desk Award. She is known for her contributions to long-form and translingual poetics, and writes in and between English and Afrikaans. Welcoming collaborative formations, her narrative poem, *Hell Light Flesh,* was adapted and produced as a mono-opera film with composer Jimmie LeBlanc, premiered at the International Festival of Films on Art in 2023. Klara develops an ongoing series of experimental and dialogic literary events called Deep Curation, an approach which posits the poetry reading as artform. *Post-Mortem of the Event* is her fourth poetry collection.